MAXIME COTON

In 2004, at the age of 18, his first collection of poetry, entitled *La Biographie de Morgane Eldä*, was published by Tétras Lyre.

Since then, in addition to numerous collaborations in magazines, he has published several books of poetry. He also develops other forms of writing (short stories, songs, theater plays).

Over the last years, Maxime Coton has been in increasing demand for poetry readings and performances in Belgium and France. In 2011 he founded Canopée, a band that mixes jazz, rock and poetry.

In order to fulfill his desire to put his energy at the service of other voices as much as his own, Coton became editor of the editions Tétras Lyre from 2009 to 2014. He launched a new collection, combining music and poetry, bringing the publishing house into the digital age.

He is relentlessly experimenting with crossovers between literature and digital media. His latest attempt to date is *Living Pages*, a Virtual Reality Poem, co-created with Paula Kehoe.

As a filmmaker, he has directed documentaries and experimental films.

Poetry

La Biographie de Morgane Eldä, Tétras Lyre, 2004
Le Geste ordinaire, Esperluète, 2011
Où votre œil s'efface, Atelier du Hanneton, 2013
L'Imparfait des langues, Arbre à paroles, 2014

Prose

Resplendir, Esperluète, 2014

Theater

L'Inondation, Lansmann Éditeur, 2014

Imperfect
tongues

Original title
L'imparfait des langues
© 2014 by L'Arbre à Paroles

English translation
© 2018 by Bruits
info@bruitsasbl.be
http://www.bruitsasbl.be
ISBN: 978-2-930828-03-9

Layout & typesetting
Sébastien Vellut – lautobus.be

Imperfect tongues

Maxime Coton

POEMS

translated from the French
by Paula Kehoe and Jean-François Sené

Bruits

Here is the story of a couple who love, eat and will die.

If we were immortal there would be no need for expression.

Reality is meaningless at the moment it ends,

This is the expression of something attained through a poem.

First, imagine that I made my way to you. A way, that through varied landscapes borrowed, would remain constant, far from language. And if it was on the island that our beings met, it is because doubt made a path where the epiphany of your face appeared triumphant.

Everything is there, in the first phonemes your shy breast carved on my pathetic hands. My fumbling steps, lit by urgency, stammered until dawn in that new country you were opening through me.

Laughter is as much a pretext as a sound. A trace of happiness the skin can hear. He makes his way to that lake (how many other lakes are witnessing our embrace?), towards that sunlit dance. It is there, at that very moment that he opens himself. Paltry echo of a music that our poor English mischievously welcomes.

Together, so to speak.

Was it that very evening? Our tongues search for themselves in their exile, extending, lengthening. You ignore the impotence of speech, searching for my sleeping sex, the expression of a blossoming love.

At night, we are the only witnesses to the surprises of your body. My powerlessness, yet, to understand it. Our story, between your thighs, in capital letters.

There is no gender in Finnish. Love, like the word 'ecstasy', does not decline in French. Search for the mistake.

I must tell of that instant hanging in a suspended landscape: its alternating mountain, sea and nothing.

I must circumscribe that long road trimmed with the ribbon of a slow waltz. Our drift towards a happiness of black pebbles, a beach like no other.

And you dance, and dance on that ageless afternoon.

The rain beats endlessly like a pulse. I give you three pebbles. Tonight you will put them under the pillow of our embrace. Your innocence will add lupins, magnolias perhaps, if I find the English translation. Out of pride, I declare myself *Your dream*. Over and over, you repeat *My dream, my dream* and roll the "Rs" until you stumble into them. I collect the shards of your voice. They will soon live in our coitus, and then in your sleep.

Now you live imagined in the first pebble. The second asks me: *Can one see beyond the eyelids? Beneath language?* The third, disbelieving, looks toward tomorrow.

I draw new countries on your back. Although your lightness surprises me, I don't say anorexia yet.

Narrating the life of your smiles, your dives into cold water, you also spell me before the disaster, the tremulation of loving words.

During the day you work barefoot. Now the evening is ours: we don't need anyone else. Wrinkled by the sun, by the heavy earth, I watch over you, wash you. I walk the soles of your feet, the hills of your ankles, I learn your skin. The geography of your body traced on the land of a thousand lakes.
" – *Is it far?*

– *You will come, won't you?"*

I come first shamelessly to the room where I find you barren. Leaping to the bench where we have not yet engraved our names.

Neither blood, nor cinder.
Neither ink, nor knives.

We have crossed the ford of being together.
Happy: an abandoned torch at last
An open secret: resignation will never be
                                in full swing.

We were a simultaneous translation,
An awkward eternity.
Interpretation of our silences,
Their rhythm: alternation of momentum
and restraint.

We understand everything, so I fear, through
the prism of the cold and the agony of our
polar land.

If therefore,

I follow the *therefore* and beyond.

Living in this jungle interior and that life,

Necessarily dense and yet,

Therefore.

I explore, I follow it

On my body it is traced

Elsewhere therefore by you.

First, the sleepless night, virgin of who knows what suspense. The kindergarten welcomes our repeated gestures so that our memories accompany the crumbled countenance. Faces forbidden from the darkness of the city. Only a lost dog accompanies the hand that searches inside you for the blonde gap. Only the wind recognises the womb of hope that blows over our cheeks.

In you, among us, binds
Something that has already happened,
Inside you, among us, joined,
We separate ourselves
From what kissing means
From the silence imposed on our unspeakable
language:

Strands of your hair, kept,
An airport carpark
Jet lag in the porthole where you watch me disappear.
Carving a farewell.

I was born in your language, on body street.
In a blast the road was traced: a revelation.
(The news travelled fast along the nerves.
Guerillas, sparks flooded the carcass.)
You drew me with your caresses.

Wearing you, I feigned heresy under my skin:
a sacred beast.

From the house of anniversaries, I was
the prodigal son. Thus, my voice wove wandering
without cease the distance to reach you,
that thread. The flame of the tongue
on the telephone was spreading.

Declaring the divergence of limbs through
punctuated voyages to the heart of the entrails.
On the school benches, you were the naked island.
Still today, I dedicate all dissections to you.

Take the tongue.

Eat it.

Eat the tongue,

Your tongue so many,

Your tongue so many times

Suspended while

Time and time again

Tempting others.

Swaying, there

Tagging the cursives of my heart.

In Brussels, in December, it was the beginning of return trips. Rather than cutting the red chord, I see you again, beyond me, supine. On a bed of silence, softness, only naked will you be yourself.

Your wound is
Your language.
You will make it ours by loving me
At the poles.

If words had dimension, I would prefer patience, a measured steeping over time, and not the voice that gives it birth. Then perhaps the full measure of our temperaments would appear. A means like any other to occupy space, the dripping heart.

You decided to play a part in my life, not in a book. So, any chronology is illusory. Every letter written, aborted, sleeping in a drawer, is of no account. Through the linear sequence of months, phone calls and shy gestures, beyond us I am searching for (what I would call to seduce you) mechanics of the sensitivities.

Your voice that grows softly from the aorta leads to silence. With its infantry procession, desire grips us by the throat. The point is not just to live, but to find the fissure, the absence of death for instance.

Time has always been a stranger to us. Or rather, being strangers to time and to our own gestures, a scribe, whose vacancy I am trying to fill here, disguised us as comets propelled towards each other. But also out of language. Out of us, a week of reprieve.

The end of the year is nothing without celebrations. The family is more welcoming to strangers. With laughter that I preserve today in fragments, you accept the gift of money in the sock drawn up your ungainly limbs. An impromptu expression of our reality made tangible by knowing gazes upon us. Like, later on, a knife.

The curtains are dresses.

Evening falls.

Night wears a fissure.

I don't want to stir up trouble, neither flushed cheeks nor conspiracy. I don't want to tangle craving. Only to plough your back with eyelashes, yes. Almost by mistake because distance proclaims the error, I'm learning love for you.

Vantaa, Vantaa, Vantaa.

I assimilate and *we* return. It is still night. Your eyelids dressed in bright colours, I start with a countdown, a parallel scene between the bedroom where your longing will welcome me soon, and the clouds, my carpet of delirium.

The difference between yesterday and the softness of your hair that my hand furrows is always elsewhere. Something unintelligible.

We have nowhere to go to, but a room and then the sky, your eyes and the snow. When a feast is shared, the preparation is exhilarating. Waiting: something tangible that the meeting won't solve, postpone and then cancel. An instant of life. Limbs know this is the price of reunion.

Comes the moment when places intertwine like hair. Gifts, postures, perfume, restaurant vouchers. A word said lower than another *Mina Rakastan Sinua* and yet it lifts us. Crossing *Merikannontie*, traces that turn us into signs. A finger that points towards yesterday where we can read palpitations, endless happiness.

We don't forget the city. The mute faces of passers-by remind me that you are here, yet not here. Every street is a reprieve. In English, without any confusion, *I miss you*. Here too, time passes. I flicker, a parasite tied to the rhythm of my beating heart. Impossible imprint of my steps over the geography of your destiny. Yet the amnesia of evening sees us reunited in quiet happiness.

The library. The school. The hospital later on.
Another school where recently you've started
learning French. The square you cross every day.

The hospital later on. The hospital, later on:
the refrain of your life.

I follow you wherever I can so that I no longer
know whether it's you or the city I love.
Every word expressed, I'm waiting. I listen
to the gaze of the passers-by.
We will soon spit on history, our old native country.

One letter is added to another,
Every sentence is a pile.
How can we, once out of the water,
Undressed, wrap ourselves
In other languages,
And find the softness of being for the other?

We set out on the dotted road, the hinge of our lives, between *Helsinki* and *Hanko* where everything seems possible that remains to be said. And if we skid, if we tear doors and blouses: the freed wheel of the crushed car. On the roof following the line, towards an endless life would you mind if I carry you?

There are words once spoken whose meaning resists the survival of dead skin. When I get bored, I eat some written by you. Indigestion has never seemed so mild, uncertainty so long. I juggle only with phonemes and the sound of your voice like a fetter. The ink settles.

If there is an eruption
Of you in my life,
There is another violent need,
An awful regret
For all of our attempts:
Love disguised as unliveable before,
From you to me
Undressed, humble, it becomes.

Tongue, centre of our desire, our discord.

The coherence of tenses is somewhat inequitable and already I should say "Miss" when I summon the imperfect to the feast of our flesh. In shreds, an accelerated life. Yet, retinal persistance tarnishes the words with a nameless violence, carrying at arm's length the sovereign image of a woman and her breath.

The gift is untranslatable,

The improbable waiting when in the world,

Trembling, everything is lacking,

Faithful to this anomaly that was us.

Our bodies part. Literature, it will continue for a time: stubborness is a long, calm river. Then life's pace will resume, the body, its doubts and its meanders. Later, the dialect of the walls will come. The silence of the other, a renewal behind which our faces elide.